Battleships

by Michael Green

Content Consultant:
Jack A. Green, Historian
Naval Historical Center

C A P S T O N E   P R E S S

M A N K A T O ,   M I N N E S O T A

C A P S T O N E   P R E S S

818 North Willow Street • Mankato, Minnesota 56001
http://www.capstone-press.com

Printed in the United States of America.

Library of Congress Cataloging-in-Publication Data
Green, Michael, 1952-
    Battleships/by Michael Green.
    p. cm. -- (Land and sea)
    Includes bibliographical references and index.
    Summary: Introduces the development, military uses, weaponry, dangers, and locomotion of battleships.
    ISBN 1-56065-554-2
    1. Battleships--United States--Juvenile literature. [1. Battleships.]
I. Title. II. Series: Land and sea (Mankato, Minn.)

V815.3.G74 1998
623.8'252—dc21

                                        97-5907
                                        CIP
                                        AC

Editorial credits
Editor, Timothy Larson; Cover design, Timothy Halldin; Illustrations,
    James Franklin; Photo Research Assistant, Michelle L. Norstad
Photo credits
Dean and Nancy Kleffman, 12
U.S. Navy, cover, 4, 6, 8, 10, 15, 17, 18, 20, 23, 24, 26, 28, 33, 34, 36, 38
    41, 47

Table of Contents

Features

Chapter 1

Battleships

Battleships are large warships. A warship is a ship with guns or other weapons that navies use for war. Until the 1940s, battleships were the most important warships in any navy. Today, all navies have replaced their battleships with aircraft carriers. An aircraft carrier is a large warship that carries planes. The U.S. Navy's last four battleships are in storage.

Battleships attacked enemy ships and destroyed enemy targets on land. To do this, navies put their largest guns on battleships. Navies also made their battleships strong to withstand attacks. Thick steel armor helped to protect battleships. Armor is a protective metal covering. Armor covered battleships and their guns.

All navies put their largest guns on battleships.

Large propellers called screws push battleships through the water.

Many countries have navies. Some navies tried to build the best battleships. When one navy built new battleships, the other navies tried to build better ones.

The U.S. Navy has built and commissioned many types of battleships. A commission is a navy order to put a ship into service. The navy named most of its battleships after states. The navy also grouped them into classes. Each class

was named after the first ship built in the group. Sometimes, a class had only one battleship in it.

Battleship Form

All modern battleships have watertight steel hulls. Watertight means completely sealed so that water cannot enter or escape. A hull is a ship's body. Battleships have two or three fitted hulls for protection. Each hull fits inside the other.

A battleship has anchors at its bow. The bow is the front of a ship. Propellers called screws are located in the stern. The stern is the rear of a ship. Screws push battleships through the water.

A battleship is divided into decks. The first deck is the top deck. People can see the top deck from outside. Sailors call the top deck, topside.

The other decks lie below the top deck. Sailors call the lower decks, below. The crew's living and work spaces are located below in rooms called compartments.

A control tower called a superstructure is located on the top deck of a battleship. The superstructure contains the bridge. The bridge is a room where the captain controls the ship. A

A battleship's superstructure contains the bridge and the ship's radar.

battleship's radar is located in the superstructure. Radar is machinery that uses radio waves to locate and guide things.

A battleship's boilers and turbines are in compartments on the lower decks. Boilers are a special kind of heater. They make steam to power the turbines. Turbines are engines. Turbines

provide the power to turn the scr[e] battleship move.

Size, Weight, Speed, and

Modern battleships are very large long as some buildings are tall. E Navy's remaining battleships is 8 meters) long. This is as long as a building is tall. These ships are th navy's history. The navy's smalle were 452 feet (136 meters) long.

Displacement describes the we Displacement is the weight of the ship pushes away from itself whil ship's displacement can change de load it carries.

The smallest U.S. Navy battles about 17,617 tons (15,855 metric The navy's remaining battleships most water. They each displace 57 (51,786 metric tons) of water.

People measure the speed of sh One knot is 1.15 miles per hour. T battleships have had top speeds of is about 40 miles (64 kilometers)

Battleship Weapons

The U.S. Navy places guns on its warships in groups. Guns that have the same size and use are placed in one set. Each set of guns is called a battery. Sailors can control and fire each battery of guns as a group. This way sailors can fire many guns at one target.

The size of some guns is given in inches. The size of other guns is given in millimeters. The inches or millimeters tell the inside width of the gun barrel.

Heavy Guns

The largest guns on U.S. Navy battleships were 16-inch guns. The navy called them heavy guns.

The largest guns on U.S. Navy battleships were the heavy, 16-inch guns.

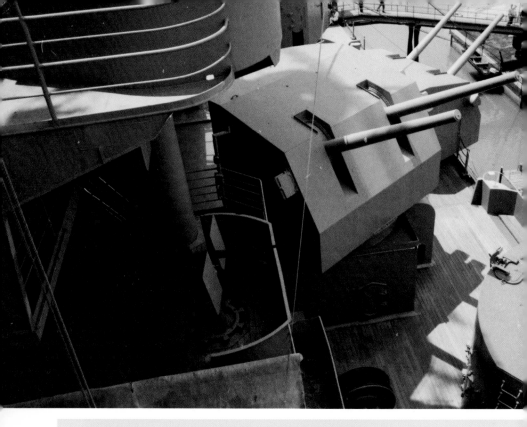

Battleships also had light, five-inch guns.

This was because they shot heavy shells. A shell is a large bullet. Each heavy shell weighed about one ton. Heavy guns on battleships fired shells as far as 24 miles (38 kilometers).

Many navy battleships carried nine heavy guns. They were mounted in three groups. Each group had three guns. These guns were called the main battery. Battleships used the main battery to attack other ships or targets on land.

Light Guns

In the 1940s, the U.S. Navy fitted its battleships with smaller, five-inch guns. The navy called the smaller guns light guns because they shot light shells. Navy battleships carried as many as 20 light guns. The navy mounted them in pairs.

The light guns on a battleship made up the secondary battery. The secondary battery guns were dual purpose. Dual purpose means used in two ways. The guns shot at enemy ships and at enemy planes.

U.S. Navy battleships also carried antiaircraft guns. Antiaircraft guns are used to shoot at attacking planes. Some of these guns were 20mm guns. Others were 40mm guns. Some battleships had as many as 75 antiaircraft guns.

Turrets and Barbettes

The U.S. Navy put the heavy and light guns in turrets. A turret is an armored shelter for guns. A turret also protects the sailors who operate the guns. A turret can move its guns from side to side. It can move them up and down. But if a battleship lost power, the turrets could not move.

The navy built many of its battleship turrets on barbettes. A barbette is a large, round tube of steel armor. Barbettes extended to the bottom of a battleship. This is where sailors stored a battleship's gun shells.

Each barbette held about 400 shells. Elevators inside the barbettes lifted the shells from the bottom of the barbettes to the turrets. In the turrets, sailors loaded the shells into the guns.

On battleships, each heavy-gun turret and barbette had a crew of about 77 sailors. They were the gun crew. Thirty of these sailors worked in the turret. The other sailors worked in the barbette. Each light-gun turret had a gun crew of 14 sailors.

Aiming the Main Battery

Before the late 1800s, sailors could not aim warship guns very well. They could not aim the guns separately. Instead, the entire ship had to turn to make the guns face their targets. This made hitting targets very difficult.

The U.S. Navy first used a turret on the battleship *Monitor* during the Civil War (1861-1865). Turrets helped sailors aim guns separately. This made it easier for navy ships to hit targets.

was named after the first ship built in the group. Sometimes, a class had only one battleship in it.

Battleship Form

All modern battleships have watertight steel hulls. Watertight means completely sealed so that water cannot enter or escape. A hull is a ship's body. Battleships have two or three fitted hulls for protection. Each hull fits inside the other.

A battleship has anchors at its bow. The bow is the front of a ship. Propellers called screws are located in the stern. The stern is the rear of a ship. Screws push battleships through the water.

A battleship is divided into decks. The first deck is the top deck. People can see the top deck from outside. Sailors call the top deck, topside.

The other decks lie below the top deck. Sailors call the lower decks, below. The crew's living and work spaces are located below in rooms called compartments.

A control tower called a superstructure is located on the top deck of a battleship. The superstructure contains the bridge. The bridge is a room where the captain controls the ship. A

A battleship's superstructure contains the bridge and the ship's radar.

battleship's radar is located in the superstructure. Radar is machinery that uses radio waves to locate and guide things.

A battleship's boilers and turbines are in compartments on the lower decks. Boilers are a special kind of heater. They make steam to power the turbines. Turbines are engines. Turbines provide the power to turn the screws to make a battleship move.

Size, Weight, Speed, and Distance

Modern battleships are very large. They are as long as some buildings are tall. Each of the U.S. Navy's remaining battleships is 887 feet (266 meters) long. This is as long as a 55-story building is tall. These ships are the largest in the navy's history. The navy's smallest battleships were 452 feet (136 meters) long.

Displacement describes the weight of ships. Displacement is the weight of the water that a ship pushes away from itself while afloat. A ship's displacement can change depending on the load it carries.

The smallest U.S. Navy battleships displaced about 17,617 tons (15,855 metric tons) of water. The navy's remaining battleships displace the most water. They each displace 57,540 tons (51,786 metric tons) of water.

People measure the speed of ships in knots. One knot is 1.15 miles per hour. The fastest navy battleships have had top speeds of 35 knots. This is about 40 miles (64 kilometers) per hour.

Battleship Weapons

The U.S. Navy places guns on its warships in groups. Guns that have the same size and use are placed in one set. Each set of guns is called a battery. Sailors can control and fire each battery of guns as a group. This way sailors can fire many guns at one target.

The size of some guns is given in inches. The size of other guns is given in millimeters. The inches or millimeters tell the inside width of the gun barrel.

Heavy Guns

The largest guns on U.S. Navy battleships were 16-inch guns. The navy called them heavy guns.

The largest guns on U.S. Navy battleships were the heavy, 16-inch guns.

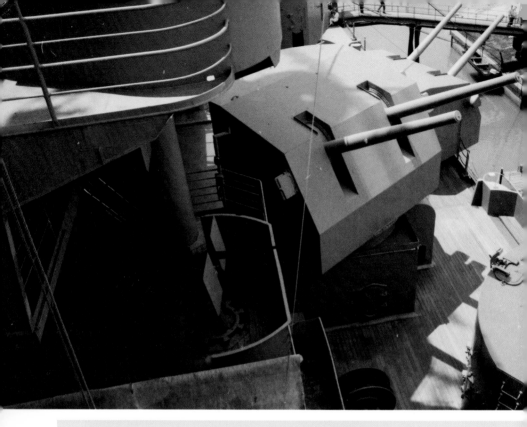

Battleships also had light, five-inch guns.

This was because they shot heavy shells. A shell is a large bullet. Each heavy shell weighed about one ton. Heavy guns on battleships fired shells as far as 24 miles (38 kilometers).

Many navy battleships carried nine heavy guns. They were mounted in three groups. Each group had three guns. These guns were called the main battery. Battleships used the main battery to attack other ships or targets on land.

Light Guns

In the 1940s, the U.S. Navy fitted its battleships with smaller, five-inch guns. The navy called the smaller guns light guns because they shot light shells. Navy battleships carried as many as 20 light guns. The navy mounted them in pairs.

The light guns on a battleship made up the secondary battery. The secondary battery guns were dual purpose. Dual purpose means used in two ways. The guns shot at enemy ships and at enemy planes.

U.S. Navy battleships also carried antiaircraft guns. Antiaircraft guns are used to shoot at attacking planes. Some of these guns were 20mm guns. Others were 40mm guns. Some battleships had as many as 75 antiaircraft guns.

Turrets and Barbettes

The U.S. Navy put the heavy and light guns in turrets. A turret is an armored shelter for guns. A turret also protects the sailors who operate the guns. A turret can move its guns from side to side. It can move them up and down. But if a battleship lost power, the turrets could not move.

The navy built many of its battleship turrets on barbettes. A barbette is a large, round tube of steel armor. Barbettes extended to the bottom of a battleship. This is where sailors stored a battleship's gun shells.

Each barbette held about 400 shells. Elevators inside the barbettes lifted the shells from the bottom of the barbettes to the turrets. In the turrets, sailors loaded the shells into the guns.

On battleships, each heavy-gun turret and barbette had a crew of about 77 sailors. They were the gun crew. Thirty of these sailors worked in the turret. The other sailors worked in the barbette. Each light-gun turret had a gun crew of 14 sailors.

Aiming the Main Battery

Before the late 1800s, sailors could not aim warship guns very well. They could not aim the guns separately. Instead, the entire ship had to turn to make the guns face their targets. This made hitting targets very difficult.

The U.S. Navy first used a turret on the battleship *Monitor* during the Civil War (1861-1865). Turrets helped sailors aim guns separately. This made it easier for navy ships to hit targets.

Each barbette housed about 400 heavy gun shells.

Radar was the most important invention for aiming weapons on U.S. Navy warships. Before radar, sailors aimed ship guns at targets using eyesight and optics. Optics are tools that magnify faraway objects. A telescope is an example of an optic tool.

Radar shows where things are located much better than eyesight and optics. It works in most weather and battle conditions. It also works over long distances. These features helped warships spot enemy targets more easily and aim their weapons better. All modern warships have radar systems.

Firing the Main Battery

The guns in a battleship's main battery could fire separately or together during a broadside. A broadside is when a ship's guns fire in one direction. This happens from either side of a ship. In one broadside, some battleships could fire nine tons (eight metric tons) of shells at a target.

The main battery guns fired two types of shells. The first was an armor-piercing shell. It could punch through the heavy armor of enemy warships. The shell exploded once it entered a part of a ship.

The second type of shell was a high-explosive shell. It contained hundreds of pounds of deadly explosives. The shell exploded when it hit something. This shell was useful against lightly armored ships and ground targets.

Battleships could fire broadsides by firing the guns of their main batteries in the same direction.

Chapter 3

Battleship History

The battleship has played an important role as a sign of naval power. The first battleships in U.S. history were built during the Civil War. The U.S. Navy built the battleship *Monitor*. The Confederate navy built the *Merrimack*. These two battleships showed the power of both navies.

Between 1906 and 1909, U.S. President Theodore Roosevelt sent 16 battleships around the world. These ships were known as the Great White Fleet. A fleet is a group of warships under one command. The fleet had this name because the navy painted the ships' hulls white. President Roosevelt used the fleet to show the growing strength of the U.S. Navy.

Battleships in the Great White Fleet had white hulls.

The U.S. Navy patterned the *Delaware* after the British battleship *Dreadnought*.

But the U.S. Navy designed its early battleships poorly. Their armor was too thin and their engines were not very powerful. Weak engines limited the battleships' speed and range. The battleships quickly became useless because of these problems.

The First Modern Battleship

In the early 1900s, the British were the best ship builders. They planned and built the first effective battleship in 1906. The British navy named the ship the *Dreadnought*.

The *Dreadnought* had 10 large guns and heavy armor. It was powered by steam turbine engines. The engines gave the ship a top speed of 21 knots. This was six knots faster than the fastest large warships at that time. The engines also increased the *Dreadnought*'s range over other battleships.

The *Dreadnought*'s advanced features made all other battleships useless. Soon, shipyards all over the world began building battleships like the *Dreadnought*.

Modern U.S. Navy Battleships

The U.S. Navy commissioned its first battleship like the *Dreadnought* in 1910. The navy named this ship the *Delaware*. The *Delaware* was 518 feet (155 meters) long and 85 feet (25.5 meters) across at its widest point.

The *Delaware* displaced more than 22,000 tons (19,800 metric tons) of water. The battleship had 10 guns. All of them were 12-inch guns. They were mounted in turrets. The turrets were protected by steel armor.

The *Delaware* was powered by steam turbine engines and had a top speed of 21 knots. It carried a crew of 933 sailors. The navy removed the *Delaware* from service in 1923. The U.S. navy scrapped the ship in 1924.

More Problems and Improvements

The navy continued to build battleships. These ships still had many design problems. The navy learned from these problems. They used the knowledge to make improvements on the next battleships that they were building.

By 1922, the Navy had 29 battleships in use or under construction. But that year, the U.S. government signed a treaty. The treaty limited the number of battleships navies could use. The navy scrapped seven of the battleships it was building to go along with the treaty.

The U.S. Navy built many new battleships until limited by a treaty signed in 1922.

Chapter 4

Fast Battleships

In 1936, the Japanese and German navies began building improved battleships. Their battleships were the world's first fast battleships. The ships carried powerful guns. The newest U.S. Navy battleship at that time was the *West Virginia*. It was built in 1923. The navy had to build more battleships to compete with the Japanese and German navies.

In 1937 and 1938, the U.S. Navy began building two battleships. Steam turbine engines gave each ship a top speed of 28 knots. This made them six knots faster than the older U.S. Navy battleships. These ships were the navy's first fast battleships.

Both fast battleships entered service in 1941. The navy named them the *North Carolina* and the *Washington*. They were part of the North Carolina class. These ships were 729 feet (219 meters) long

The Japanese navy began building improved battleships in 1936. They completed the battleship *Yamato* in 1941.

The *Missouri* entered service in the 1940s.

and 108 feet (32 meters) wide. They displaced up to
35,000 tons (31,500 metric tons) of water. Each
ship had a crew of about 1,880 sailors.

The North Carolina class battleships were armed
with nine heavy guns. The guns were arranged in
sets of three in turrets. They were also armed with
20 light guns. These guns were mounted in turrets
in sets of two.

South Dakota Class

By 1940, the U.S. Navy began construction on an
improved type of fast battleship. These ships were

the *South Dakota*, the *Indiana*, the *Massachusetts*, and the *Alabama*. All four of these ships were part of the South Dakota class.

The South Dakota class battleships had heavier armor than older battleships. The navy hoped this would make them stand up better against enemy attacks. They had a top speed of 27 knots, even with heavier armor. Each ship had a crew of 2,354 sailors.

Iowa Class Battleships

The U.S. Navy commissioned its last battleships in the 1940s. The ships are the *Iowa*, the *New Jersey*, the *Wisconsin*, and the *Missouri*. These ships are fast battleships. They are in the Iowa class.

The ships in this class are the largest battleships ever built for the navy. They are 887 feet (266 meters) long and 108 feet (32 meters) wide. Steam turbine engines power these ships. They each have an average speed of 33 knots. They can carry crews of up to 2,800 sailors.

More than 10,000 tons (9,000 metric tons) of armor covers these ships. The sides of their hulls are 12 inches (30 centimeters) thick. Their three heavy gun turrets are protected by 18 inches (45 centimeters) of armor. The ships are currently in storage.

Chapter 5

Battleships at War

On December 7, 1941, Japanese planes attacked Pearl Harbor. Pearl Harbor was the home of the U.S. Navy's Pacific Fleet. Eight battleships were in the harbor that day.

The Japanese used 360 planes launched from aircraft carriers to attack Pearl Harbor. Their planes attacked the U.S. Navy's battleships and sank four of them. These battleships were the *Arizona*, the *Oklahoma*, the *West Virginia*, and the *California*.

U.S. sailors beached the battleship *Nevada* to prevent it from sinking. Beach means to move a ship into shallow water. The *Maryland* and the *Tennessee* suffered only light bomb damage. The

Sailors used antiaircraft guns to defend battleships from attacking planes during the attack on Pearl Harbor.

Pennsylvania was in dry dock. A dry dock is a large dock for storing ships out of the water. Only one bomb hit the ship.

After the attack on Pearl Harbor, the United States entered World War II (1939-1945). Except for the *Arizona* and the *Oklahoma*, the navy rebuilt its damaged battleships. The rebuilt battleships returned to service during the war.

Battleship Against Battleship

In November 1942, the Japanese sent a large fleet of ships to Guadalcanal. Guadalcanal is an island in the Pacific Ocean. The island was protected by U.S. Navy ships. The Japanese fleet's job was to sink the U.S. Navy's ships.

The meeting of the two fleets led to one of the best-known battles of World War II. This battle was part of a naval campaign known as the Guadalcanal Campaign. A campaign is a series of battles. Campaigns can last days or even months.

On November 14, two U.S. Navy battleships spotted the Japanese battleship *Kirishima*. The American battleships were the *Washington* and the *South Dakota*.

The *South Dakota* sank a Japanese destroyer that was with the *Kirishima*. A destroyer is a

The U.S. Navy started using battleships with other warships to protect its aircraft carriers.

small warship. But the Japanese also damaged the *South Dakota* and caused its power to fail. The *South Dakota* could not use its heavy guns. It had to leave the battle. The *Washington* fought the rest of the battle on its own.

The *Washington*'s main battery fired 75 heavy shells at the *Kirishima*. Nine of them hit the *Kirishima*. They knocked out the ship's engines. The *Kirishima* caught on fire. Four hours later, the Japanese abandoned their ship, and it sank.

Protecting Aircraft Carriers

By 1943, the U.S. Navy decided to use its battleships with other warships to protect its aircraft carriers. The navy realized that aircraft carrier planes were better weapons than battleship guns. The planes could attack targets on land and on water more easily.

The U.S. Navy's battleship the *North Carolina* was a battleship that protected aircraft carriers. It protected the aircraft carriers the *Enterprise* and the *Hornet* during naval battles.

Japanese planes tried to attack the *Enterprise* in late August 1942. The *North Carolina* used its antiaircraft guns to shoot them down.

In mid-October 1942, the *North Carolina* was protecting the aircraft carrier *Hornet*. A Japanese torpedo fired at the *Hornet*, but hit the *North Carolina* instead. A torpedo is an explosive that can travel underwater. It tore a 32-foot (10-meter) hole in the battleship. But the *North Carolina* kept on fighting. The two ships defeated the Japanese planes.

The navy repaired the *North Carolina* and used the ship until 1947. The ship is now a museum in Wilmington, North Carolina.

World War II Naval Battles of the Pacific Ocean

1. Pearl Harbor,
   Dec. 7,1941
2. Battle of the Coral Sea,
   May 4-8, 1942
3. Battle of Midway,
   June 3-6, 1942
4. Guadalcanal Campaign,
   Aug. 7, 1942 to Feb. 21, 1943

5. Northern Solomons Campaign,
   Feb. 22,1943 to Nov 21, 1944
6. Battle of the Komandorski Islands,
   March 26, 1943
7. Truk Attack,
   Feb. 17-18, 1944
8. Battle of the Philippine Sea,
   June 19-20, 1944
9. Leyte Campaign,
   Oct. 17, 1944 to July 1,1945
10. Sinking of the Yamato,
    April 7, 1945
11. Destruction of the Japanese navy,
    July 10 to Aug. 15, 1945

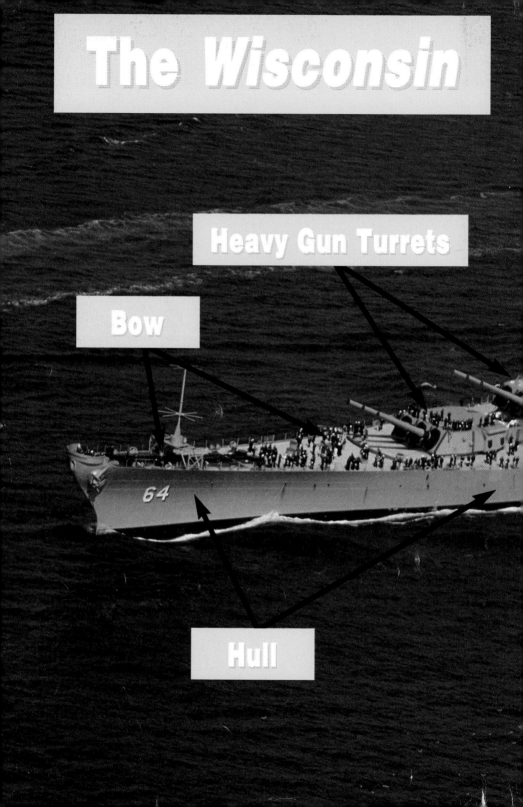

**Bridge**

Superstructure

Heavy Gun Turret

Stern

Hull

**Light Gun Turrets**

Chapter 6

Safety and the Future

Battleships and their crews faced many dangers. Enemy warships, submarines, and planes tried to sink them during battle. There was also the chance for accidents because of all the weapons battleships carried. Safety features were built into battleships.

A battleship's most important safety feature was its armor. Thick armor protected the ship, its weapons, and its crew from enemy attacks. The armor on many navy battleships ranged from six inches (15 centimeters) to 18 inches (45 centimeters) thick.

A battleship's fitted hulls also provided protection for the battleship and its crew. The

Armor protected a battleship, its weapons, and its crew members.

hulls made it harder for enemy explosives to blow holes in the ship. This kept a battleship from sinking. If an outer hull was damaged, an inner hull kept water out of the ship.

During battle, sailors on a battleship wore helmets. The helmets protected their heads from bullets. They also wore life jackets. Life jackets help people float in water. The sailors also wore life jackets when the sea was rough. Ship doctors cared for injured and sick sailors.

Defensive Weapons

On battleships, antiaircraft guns were the most important weapons for defense. Defend means to protect from harm. By the late 1940s, improved planes and weapons made these guns less useful. The improved planes were fast and fired powerful missiles. A missile is an explosive that can fly long distances. The planes were too fast for the guns. Battleship antiaircraft guns could not shoot down the planes. The navy needed a better weapon.

In the 1960s, weapons experts developed the 20mm Phalanx antimissile gun system. The Phalanx weapon system has a gun with six

Sailors on battleships wore helmets during battle.

barrels. The gun is connected to radar and a computer. The radar and computer work together to spot planes and aim the gun. This all happens within seconds. The gun can fire up to 3,000 shots per minute.

In the 1980s, the navy put cruise missiles on its remaining battleships. A cruise missile is a missile with an on-board computer. The computer in the missile helps guide it toward a target. Some cruise missiles can hit targets more than 1,000 miles (1,600 kilometers) away.

The End of the Line

After 1945, the U.S. Navy scrapped most of its battleships. A few became museums. The navy only kept its four Iowa class battleships. These ships spend most of their time in storage.

Since then, the navy has brought the Iowa class battleships out of storage three times. The navy used all four battleships during the Korean War (1950-1952). The *New Jersey* came out of storage during the Vietnam War (1965-1975). And the *Wisconsin* and the *Missouri* took part in Operation Desert Storm (1991).

The U.S. Navy put cruise missiles on its battleships in the 1980s.

In 1995, the navy decided it no longer needed battleships. No one knows what will happen to the four remaining Iowa class battleships. The navy wants to donate the ships to museums. So far, only the *Missouri* may have found a permanent home. People at Pearl Harbor want to make the ship a public museum.

Words to Know

armor (AR-mur)—a protective metal covering

barbette (BARB-et)—a large, round tube of steel armor that extended from a turret to the bottom of a battleship

beach (BEECH)—to move a ship into shallow water

boiler (BOI-lur)—a special heater that makes steam to power turbines

bridge (BRIJ)—the room where the captain controls a ship

broadside (BRAWD-side)—when a ship fires all its guns in the same direction

cruise missile (KROOZ MISS-uhl)—a type of missile that steers itself to a target using an on-board computer

destroyer (di-STROI-ur)—a small warship used for hunting submarines

dry dock (DRYE DOK)—a large dock for storing ships out of the water

fleet (FLEET)—a group of warships under one command

hull (HUHL)—the body of a ship

knot (NOT)—a measurement of speed for ships and boats; 1.15 miles per hour

missile (MISS-uhl)—an explosive that can fly long distances

radar (RAY-dar)—machinery that uses radio waves to locate and guide things

submarine (SUHB-muh-reen)—a ship that can travel both on top of water and underwater

torpedo (tor-PEE-doh)—an explosive that travels underwater

turbine (TUR-bine)—an engine powered by steam, water, or gas

turret (TUR-it)—an armored shelter for guns

warship (WOR-ship)—a ship with guns or other weapons that navies use for war

To Learn More

Asimov, Isaac and Elizabeth Kaplan. *How Do Big Ships Float?* Milwaukee: Gareth Stevens, 1993.

Newhart, Max R. *American Battleships*. Missoula, Mont.: Pictorial Histories Publishing Company, 1995.

Preston, Antony. *Battleships*. Greenwich, Conn.: Bison Books, 1982.

Sullivan, George. *Return of the Battleship*. New York: Dodd, 1983.

Useful Addresses

Battleship *Texas*
3527 Battleground Road
La Porte, TX 77571

Naval Historical Center
Washington Navy Yard
901 M Street SE
Washington, DC 20374-5060

U.S.S. *Alabama* **Battleship Commission**
Battleship Parkway
P.O. Box 65
Mobile, AL 36601

U.S.S. *North Carolina* **Battleship Memorial**
P.O. Box 480
Wilmington, NC 28402

Internet Sites

Comprehensive Battleship Lists
http://www.membrane.com:80/~elmer/navy/battleships

Guided Missiles
http://www.nawcwpns.navy.mil:80/clmf/bat.html

Iowa Class Preservation Association
http://www.endif.com:80/icpa/icpa.html

Navy: Welcome Aboard
http://www.navy.mil/

The *New Jersey* last came out of storage during the Vietnam War. It is shown here just after firing a missile.

Index